# A SUGGESTED BLUEPRINT FOR SINGLE MOTHER PARENTING

# A SUGGESTED BLUEPRINT

# FOR

# SINGLE MOTHER PARENTING

Michele Vaughn, Ed.D.

*A Suggested Blueprint for Single Mother Parenting*
*All Rights Reserved.*
Copyright © 2016 Dr. Michele Vaughn

Published by Mackenzie Publishing
Edited by C.A. MacKenzie
Halifax, Nova Scotia
ISBN-13: 978-1927529362
ISBN-10: 1927529360

The opinions expressed in this manuscript are solely the opinions of the author and do not represent the opinions or thoughts of the publisher. The author has represented and warranted full ownership and/ or legal right to publish all the materials in this book.

To Book the Author for a book signing & speaking session, send your request to **www.drmv.net** by clicking on the request speaking services or email **drmvspeak@gmail.com**.

This book may not be reproduced, transmitted, or stored in whole or in part by any means, including graphic, electronic, or mechanical without the express written consent of the publisher except in the case of brief quotations embodied in critical articles and reviews.

ఞ⚜ఞ
MacKenzie Publishing

# Introduction

**A** "blueprint" is defined as a designed plan or other technical drawing. It is meant to provide a preview of a suggested end result with intricate details of what is needed to accomplish the goal.

The suggested blueprint provided in this booklet is deliberately focused on single mother parenting with every intention to build up, provide guidance, encourage, and uplift the life of a single mother parent who has the responsibility of raising a child to become a responsible and productive human being. As a former pregnant teen, divorcee, and striving single mother, it has been a strong conviction of mine to share successful parenting tips as I have navigated my way through life to become self-sufficient and be a positive role model to my two sons.

The journey of parenting does not come with a perfect manual, which simply means that each parent must gain experience through subjective trial and error. As single mothers, we have to touch base with our past and examine the tools our parents (or legal guardians) used when we were growing up. I like to refer to this as "Parenting Unpacking," which literally involves a mother sorting through what she deemed as appropriate parenting versus what was not, while she mimics certain traits acquired from her parents in her single mother parenting undertaking.

The concepts expressed in this booklet are to serve as a help and not a hindrance, and much of the parenting tips are derived from my personal journey as a single mother parent, along with my interactions with other mothers who have the challenge of raising the next generation on their own.

It is my hope that you are able to glean what you need from this booklet and walk away with a new harvest of inspirational parenting!

# Table of Contents

| | |
|---|---|
| Blueprint Tip One<br>Deconstruct and Rebuild | 1 |
| Blueprint Tip Two<br>What Are Your Parenting Expectations | 5 |
| Blueprint Tip Three<br>Parenting Communication | 9 |
| Blueprint Tip Four<br>Bypassing Toxic Relationships to Safeguard Your Child | 14 |
| Blueprint Tip Five<br>Crafting a Self-Sufficiency Plan | 19 |
| Blueprint Tip Six<br>Become Involved in Your Child's Education | 23 |
| Blueprint Tip Seven<br>Spiritual Soup for the Soul | 27 |
| Blueprint Tip Eight<br>Be What You Want to See | 30 |
| Closing Parent Declaration | 33 |
| Your Blueprint Initial Thoughts | 34 |
| Meet the Author, Dr. Michele Vaughn | 36 |
| Additional Readings by Dr. MV | 39 |

## Blueprint Tip One
## Deconstruct and Rebuild

The term "deconstruct" is defined as to reduce something to its constituent parts in order to reinterpret it. As it relates to parenting, there is no perfect example and there are no absolutes of what is perfectly defined as good and bad parenting. There are only subjective experiences that become a part of our adopted concept of what parenting should or should not be.

In order to create a foundation of parenting you can build on and trust that the decisions you make will produce a great harvest in your child's character, I believe a deconstruction phase is most necessary. What is this and how does this look for a single mother? This is where a mother intentionally takes time to deal with her past as it pertains to her upbringing and sorts through the various experiences she had growing up with her parents or legal guardian.

This process does not feel good nor is it pretty, but it is necessary if the mother desires to implement healthy parenting to her child. Oftentimes, single mothers do not take the time to reflect on their childhood upbringing with the intention of sorting through past conflicts simply because they tend to parent in "survival mode." They don't redeem the time in a manner that will produce a greater reflection of who they can become versus staying stuck with who they are, which can be attributed to a sum result of their past experiences.

To begin the "deconstruction" process, I always suggest to single mother parents to do this by way of journaling. As a single mother myself, I started the deconstruction phase when I had my first son twenty years ago.

This process was not something anyone suggested to me, but it was a way I was able to hear my own thoughts and revisit my thinking and develop a communication line between God and me. It was important for me to date every journal entry because this served as a benchmark of progression moving forward in life, reviewing where I was on the same day two or three years later. Did I grow spiritually? Was I still stuck with the same prohibiting thoughts? Did I mature in certain areas that were once great challenges for me?

This is the primary tool I would suggest to any single mother parent who is beginning the deconstruction phase: pick up a notepad and a pen and remain consistent in order to dig through the pile of accumulated rubble that has formed in your soul. It is quite possible that you will feel vulnerable and sad during this time due to the sensitivity of the past content you have addressed in your writings. It may serve you well to include a trusted individual (pastor, counselor, psychologist, or close friend) who will help you navigate through tough memories and not judge you in the process but, rather, encourage you to see the benefit factor moving forward.

Your rebuilding begins when you decide that deconstruction is necessary if your blueprint parenting model is one that you hope will produce healthy parenting for your child and a great parenting experience for you as a single mother.

### Dr. MV's Blueprint Tip

If you don't take the time to deconstruct now and press pause in life to create a space called "serving me," the risk of unhealthy and frustrated parenting will serve as your portion. I never said this would be easy, but trust me, it is so worth it!

# Blueprint Tip Two
# What Are Your Parenting Expectations?

Every building, home, school, church, and road that was ever created first started with a blueprint. Engineers, architects, and construction workers all work together on a single project in order to produce the expected end results.

Single mother parenting is not much different with the exception of the mother serving as the chief visionary of the blueprint. Much of the work and sweat equity involved in achieving the parenting outcomes desired is related to dealing with oneself from the inside out.

The unfortunate reality is there are so many single mothers who did not plan to become mothers, but due to a passionate night of physical intimacy, the result of that small moment in time produced a lifetime of expectations and responsibilities. And because the pregnancy was not planned and resources and proper support were not available, the single mother is now in a position in life that forces her to think outside of herself and make the right decisions concerning the growth of another human being. This can definitely create pressure that can be almost unbearable if the proper mindset is not challenged to activate itself early on to establish set parenting expectations.

For example, when I was a young single mother after my divorce and raising two sons alone at the age of 24, I made clear decisions on the type of woman and mother I wanted to be, decisions that would cost me old friendships, fun nights out, limited dating, etc. It was important for me to discover who the greater me was even though my parenting was at a freshman level. My big idea suggested that if I altered my lifestyle and set goals for myself as a mother, this would add much value to the lives of my two boys growing up.

As a parent it is our duty to establish set expectations—not only for ourselves but for our children as well. Without set expectations, you will encounter what I like to call "loose parenting": simply put, an "anything goes" type of parenting, creating a cycle of confusion and instability for your child.

Being a mother is not just in title or responsibility but is a position that puts you in a creational place to speak life, inspire the next generation, and demonstrate unconditional love to a human being depending upon you for clear directions in life. You can't successfully parent alone without setting expectations in various areas of your life and what you desire from your child. It is like having a full tank of gas in your car with a goal of driving from Illinois to Florida. Without a map (directions) to get there, you are simply wasting gas.

Parenting requires a blueprint that helps you navigate through various decisions connected to your mothering.

## Dr. MV's Blueprint Tip

Create the intentional time to set expectations for yourself as a single mother and hold yourself accountable in fulfilling them. It is okay to include an accountability person on this journey as long as their motive is to help you reach your parenting goals.

# Blueprint Tip Three
# Parenting Communication

Communication! Communication! Communication! What is it? How does it sound? How should it be interpreted? Does it have a look? So many questions regarding the art of communication and the effectiveness it has between two individuals or a group.

As single mothers, we have a voice that can resonate with our child unlike anybody else's on the planet. This traces back to when you were carrying your child during pregnancy and the various developmental stages the fetus went through over a process of months.

Research suggests that at week twenty-four, hearing is activated and your unborn baby is able to hear voices and sounds in the outside world. But mainly, they are connected to a unique voice they hear daily, a voice that will carry them through their lives once they enter the world, and that is the voice of their mother!

Every mother has her own sound, her own tone, her own way of communicating to her child that either uplift or discourage. Parenting communication is very subjective and cannot be compared from household to household, but there should be at some point a willingness from the single mother to establish the type of acceptable communication language she will incorporate into her healthy blueprint parenting model.

So let's travel back to the "parenting unpacking" process, which should have allowed you to review the type of communication you grew up listening to with your parent or legal guardian. Did you experience negative communication styles (i.e., cursing and negative name-calling, etc.)?

No household is totally exempt from negative parenting communication because there are no perfect human beings on the planet. And let's be real: parenting can be tough, but this is

not an excuse to use words as a weapon of war with people you love.

Another negative parenting communication that can be displayed to your child if you are not careful is giving your child "the silent treatment": no communication at all or totally ignoring your child and not acknowledging his or her presence in the room.

When you begin to really think about negative parenting communication, this can create emotional gaps in children's lives that will lead them down a path of searching for reaffirming voices from others who may not mean them any good in life. Because they thirst for words of life spoken to them, they bypass the red flags in a person's character to receive a sip of positive spoken dialogue and to be understood. This is how kids can easily choose the wrong crowd in school or friendships.

As a single mother, your voice is of the utmost importance and not to be taken lightly. When you choose to use your words to build up your child's thoughts about himself or herself and speak words that will make him or her feel like he or she just drank a fresh cup of cold water, you are setting the tone for what is acceptable language and what is not.

As children grow up, they will encounter their own relationship experiences and must make decisions. Certain choices they make will not speak to the quality of life you desire for them but a lesson to be learned.

Your child will not be perfect, but with positive parenting, if you take the time to demonstrate what is appropriate and what is not appropriate, the child will have a foundation to convince him or her otherwise when a powerful negative opposite is encountered. But if you are the negative force and choose to use degrading communication, the responsibility of the outcome of who the child becomes when older will have to be acknowledged by you. You may not like that, but it is the truth.

I believe, as a single mother, it is important we model the best way we possibly can. This may include apologizing to your child when you have spoken in a negative manner. I have had to do this in my early single parenting because I simply was just learning how to use the tool of positive communication.

Negative communication is like misspelled signs on the road. Instead of "stop," which is meant to give us caution, you read "No one is looking, so go anyway."

One time, I overheard a mother cursing at her little son who was jumping around and not listening to her, and because she was frustrated and possessed no control, she used her words as a tool (hammer) to beat him down.

My skin crawls whenever I hear parents curse at their child! In creating your healthy parenting blueprint, positive communication is an important key to examine which has the power to serve as the "master key" in your child's life, unlocking treasures within that will position the child to prosper in the various stages of development. Speak Life!

### Dr. MV's Blueprint Tip

You have the power to change the direction of your child's future by the way in which you choose to communicate. Use your voice wisely and speak to your child how you want to be spoken to!

# Blueprint Tip Four
# Bypassing Toxic Relationships to Safeguard Your Child

**A**s a single mother, whether you accept it or not, your child looks to you to create the blueprint and expectations regarding the various relationships we are to have in our lives. Ultimately, if your child is in your care over 50 percent of the time, you have the primary obligation to determine what is acceptable and what is not.

If you are a single mom due to divorce or a single mom due to a physical intimate moment with someone and now have the sole responsibility of raising a child, you must be cautious who you allow around your child. Think of it this way: If you were seeking directions from someone who provided a pathway that consisted of potholes, orange cones, and detours, would you still be committed to staying on that path, or would you seek an alternative route without the caution signs?

I hope you wouldn't try to force your way down a pathway that was clearly under construction and, instead, hope you'd find an alternative route with less drama. The same is true for relationships and exposing your child to healthy and unhealthy characters.

If you have taken the time to go through the process of "deconstruction," you uncovered childhood pain, dealt with anger, and sorted through acceptable and unacceptable parenting behavior you encountered growing up. You are literally setting a new foundation of expectations as a single mother and head of household for your child. All of this mental and spiritual sweat equity is not in vain and requires that you continue perfecting your blueprint parenting model by dealing with relationships.

I would like to think we all have experienced relationships that were considered to be toxic, which is no good in the end and takes us out of our element in a negative manner and leaves us in a destitute state of being. As a single mother, your goal should be to assess the different relationships you have embraced (friends, associates, professionals, spiritual, and romantic).

Why is this key? Your child is still developing mentally and physically with the model example of you as protector of his or her well-being. Granted, if you are single, there is a large chance you will become lonely at some point in parenting and desire a mate, but this desire should not make you close your eyes to red flags when encountering different candidates for you and your child as it relates to a potential husband. You are no longer choosing for yourself; you are choosing for you and your child, which means your decision making is "selfless" not "selfish."

Also, let me point out the difference between feeling lonely, which is sadness, and being alone, which is physically being by oneself.

Oftentimes, single mothers have not taken the time to set goals and create a healthy parenting blueprint and will select a guy in their lives simply because they have yet to enjoy their own company and accomplish goals, which take up major time in a single day and season. The best relationship you could ever establish as a single mother is with the one you carried for nine months—your child. When you create time to spend outside of what may appear to be parenting duties (the routine) with your child (i.e., walk in the park, go for ice cream, swim at the pool, enjoy fun games at home, etc.), this allows you as a mother to discover your child's gifts, skills, and talents because this time is enjoyable and not duty associated. This time also teaches your child that he or she plays an important role in your life, and you are teaching the child the other side of parenting by spending quality time outside of the daily routine.

In my own single mothering, I took my sons to the park or took them bowling or took them for ice cream, to enjoy and experience another side of their personalities I didn't see in our day-to-day routine. The relationships you allow in your life as a single mother should be relationships that will complement the blueprint you deem as acceptable. If the person you are entertaining has red flags and orange cones around them (figuratively speaking, of course), by all means heed to the signs and don't create an imaginable green light with the mindset of "I can change them" or "They are not that bad." The last thing you need for your child is to have a traumatic experience with a stranger due to your unwillingness to walk away early on!

**Dr. MV Blueprint Tip**

Exposing your child to toxic relationships will do more harm than good in their development, and it is up to you as a single mother to ensure that no poison is introduced on purpose to your child through your associations. Protect Your Child!

# Blueprint Tip Five
# Crafting a Self-Sufficiency Plan

The traditional concept of "self-sufficiency" is defined as needing no outside help with supporting one's basic needs in life. But it can go further to explore ideas of being emotionally and intellectually independent.

As a single mother, you have the responsibility to raise your child and not only monitor behavior, character development, model integrity, and acceptable forms of communication but also to provide the necessities in life (food, shelter, clothing, and basic education).

For a young single mother, these responsibilities can seem overwhelming and almost impossible. But I believe if you start early with your parenting blueprint creation, your self-sufficiency is attainable.

Can we agree with the concept that no one decides when they are young that they want to become a failure when they become an adult? I believe the hurdles that life presents many of us are there to shape our character and not to haunt us with dark thoughts beginning with "I can't" throughout our adult life. Parenting is not easy, and we all need a support system to help us navigate through the various stages of parenting, which makes single mother parenting "interdependent" on others who will support you. There is a difference between asking for a hand-out versus a hand-up. In my profession working with single mothers, we promote the hand-up mentality.

Crafting a self-sufficiency plan will require your time, your thoughts, your goals, and mainly your self-worth! When you position yourself in a place that allows you the freedom to create a roadmap of success, this then allows your child to witness up close and personal what goal setting looks like and how accomplishing a goal creates a stronger sense of self-worth.

When you operate at a high level of self-worth, this decreases the chances of accepting toxic relationships and you then become particular about your affiliations and surroundings.

Your self-sufficiency doesn't necessarily mean you don't need help because, let's face it, everybody needs somebody to help them along the way, but it gives you a sense of personal direction. As a single mother, you can still dream and move forward in a way with your child to accomplish your dream. If that dream is obtaining a college degree or buying a home or paying off your debt, it is possible. As the Chief Designer of your parenting blueprint, you have the power to engraft your dream of self-sufficiency into the plan.

Don't limit yourself because of your circumstances. Where you are right now is called the end of a particular chapter, not the end of your story!

### Dr. MV's Blueprint Tip

Crafting a plan to succeed with deadlines will help you reach your goals. Don't settle for less because you are a single mother. If anything, this should make you strive that much harder to create a positive blueprint of success.

# Blueprint Tip Six
# Become Involved in
# Your Child's Education

When it comes to education, I personally believe it is critical to remain in the loop with your child's progress or lack thereof. But for a single mother who is working two jobs with barely enough time in a day to create a sense of normal, this can become a challenge. For the single mother who did not complete a high school diploma or a GED, the feeling of inadequacy may overwhelm and create a distance between you and your child's education.

Here is what I suggest from one single mother to another: It matters not your current level of education completion, but your willingness to engage with your child's learning process as he or she goes from grade to grade. This close-up involvement will speak volumes to your child as it relates to your set expectations of your child and the importance of education in your home.

If you think about how long your child spends with his or her teacher throughout the day along with, perhaps, after school care, when the child finally arrives home, your presence is limited, but all it requires is a conversation about school over dinner. The conversation may sound like this: *How was school today? What did you learn? Can I see your homework before you go to bed?*

Although you both may be tired due to activities of the day, remember your voice is the primary voice that will create a sense of direction for your child. Try to deliver this conversation in a light manner and pleasant tone versus a demanding demeanor or what can appear to be fearful on the child's end.

When I was a young mom, I didn't know how to communicate in this manner and would approach my sons with an unnecessary intenseness that intimidated them. I felt pressure from the day of working and going to school at night, and internally my parental thoughts were that maybe I was neglecting my sons because of the limited time we had together.

Never displace your ill feelings onto your child because it can cause more damage than good. Eventually, I became heavily involved in my sons' education and made sure that no matter what my schedule was, being at parent meetings, volunteering for field trips, and other afterschool functions were nonnegotiable as it related to anything or anyone that interfered with my involvement.

As a single mother, you have the power to speak life into your child's future by letting him or her know how brilliant, smart, and intelligent he or she is and your expectation for him or her to produce his or her best work when it comes to education. Even if grades look the opposite of your positive praise, speaking positive—despite what the situation looks like—empowers your child's ability to perform at his or her best level because he or she knows his or her main cheerleader is at home waiting.

## Dr. MV's Blueprint Tip

Education first starts at home. What you teach in your home is the beginning of how your child will respond to the formal education system. Get involved!

# Blueprint Tip Seven
# Spiritual Soup for the Soul

I recall when my sons became under the weather during the winter months. The first thing I did was supplement their meal plan with chicken noodle soup. It was something about the ease of preparing soup that brought calmness to their coughing and sneezing. Of course, medication was used as well, but their main meal while under the weather would be chicken noodle soup.

When it comes to parenting, I believe, outside of the expected responsibilities to provide the necessities for your child (i.e., food, clothes, shelter, and basic education), there is also a need to adopt a spiritual model to assist in creating the foundation of moral excellence. Our children will model what they see inside the home and mimic a display of their upbringing in public. The core principles of life, I believe, are narrated in a spiritual concept adopted in their early years of development through the teaching of their parent.

For my household, our personal spiritual foundation derives from a Christian background whereby the teaching of Jesus Christ is the premiere example for moral excellence. My sons have watched their mother pray, read the bible, attend fellowship, and implement various concepts displayed in the written Word of God. As a single mother, I find it challenging to believe that we, by nature, can be carriers of life and not carry a Word in us that will deliver a powerful message of hope, restoration, and empowerment to our offspring.

When your child struggles with decision-making due to peer pressure or the basic issues of life, you as a parent are looked to as the primary "go to" person to apply chicken noodle soup for the soul. There must be a remedy to help children navigate through that difficult challenge in life that has much to do with the shaping of their character.

If your child is challenged in school to adopt a certain lifestyle that doesn't sit well with his or her spirit and the child comes to you for advice, outside of your subjective opinion as a mother, what will be your foundation for moral excellence? What is acceptable and what is not? How do you shape your standards for right or wrong character traits? See my point? I am trying to simply suggest that every single mother should adopt a spiritual foundation that will help shape the direction for moral excellence in raising a child.

**Dr. MV's Blueprint Tip**

Say a prayer of protection, guidance, and encouragement with your children every single day. This action will inspire them to believe in the power of their creational purpose.

## Blueprint Tip Eight
## Be What You Want to See

**W**hile single mother parenting can be tough, especially if you have limited support and raising the opposite sex (son), there is a great chance you can still model acceptable behavior that will produce a responsible and respectable child. While you are not a man and do not possess the qualities or features of a man, there is power in your ability to tap into the woman/nurturing side of being a mother.

When you think of a mirror and its purpose, which is to give an exact replica of who you are while standing in front of it, the same concept can be applied to single mother parenting. Your child is a mirror reflection of you! Some of us may not like this statement for various reasons, but the majority of what I am suggesting has valid truth if we are totally honest.

Children do as they see us do, not so much what they hear us say. If you desire that your child is respectable to adults, it is going to require you to treat the waiter with respect or speak nicely over the phone to the bill collector (although this can be a challenge). If you want your children to respect their teachers in school, it is going to require you to let your children know the importance of education and feel your involvement regarding their academics. If you want your child to have integrity, it is also going to mean that they watch you do the right thing when no one is looking.

My point is that we, as single mothers, must take ownership of our child's upbringing and not place blame outside of what we can control in our homes. While our child may be influenced by outsiders, their foundational teaching, which is of the utmost importance, will come from the mirror reflection of what they see from their mother.

A single mother wants to avoid what I like to call "crack parenting," which refers to an emotionally damaged or bruised mother who displaces this same abuse to her child. This is a mother who was not raised properly and did not take the time to deal with her issues. She speaks ill to her child and uses words as weapons of mass destruction versus using her words as a powerful tool to build up her child who could possibly become the next president one day.

This is why it is key to do your parenting unpacking early to assess what is appropriate and what is not. You have the power to serve in the role of an accomplished mother, no longer pointing the finger at what you didn't have growing up but taking ownership of what is possible moving forward and projecting those abilities to your child.

### Dr. MV's Blueprint Tip

Speak words of life to your child and live a life you can be proud of behind closed doors and in the public. Remember, your child is very smart and mimics everything you say and do!

# Closing Parent Declaration

**I** admit that being a single mother is challenging on a daily basis, but it is not out of my reach to be the best mother to my child that I can possibly be. While I may not have come from the best background, I will not allow this to serve as an excuse to not try to provide the best upbringing for my child.

From this day forward, I decree and declare that I will do the work needed from the inside out and pursue my purpose that will ultimately build up my family and bring us to a place we can be proud of. I am not a victim, but I stand in the place of victory because giving birth to my child was not by accident. I will not allow my child's life to serve as a punishment for living but, rather, a celebration for existing. I am blessed, and the blueprint I create will be one that my children's children will talk about for generations to come!

I am a phenomenal single mother; yeah, that's me!

# Your Blueprint Initial Thoughts

# Meet the Author
# Dr. Michele Vaughn

Dr. Michele Vaughn is an Entrepreneur, Author, Inspirational Speaker, Leadership Trainer, and Coach. She currently serves in dual roles as the Founder & CEO of the Teen & Single Mother Resource Center, Inc. as well as the Founder of Lead 2 Inspire Training Institute with a John C. Maxwell Certification. Her primary mission for single mothers is to empower them to become a positive role model to their children through the power of advanced education.

Much of Dr. Vaughn's passion in the field of education and human service stems from her own past struggle as a college dropout who was labeled as "just another pregnant teen." She refused to surrender to the pressures of rejection, suicide, and uncertainty by making a decision to complete her education and become a well-equipped role model to her two sons.

Today, Dr. Vaughn has earned an Associate of Arts Degree from the College of Lake County, a Bachelor Degree in Psychology from Columbia College of Missouri, a Master of

Science Degree in Counseling from Capella University, and a Doctorate in Educational Leadership at Argosy University. Currently Dr. Vaughn travels as a leadership trainer and speaker as a Certified John C. Maxwell team member working with schools, non-profits, and other businesses.

In addition, she recently published her second book, titled *BRIDE* (Becoming Royal in Daddy's Eyes), which speaks to singles seeking companionship. She is also launching professional leadership workshops and conferences through her company Lead 2 Inspire Training Institute for aspiring leaders working in diverse settings.

Dr. Vaughn is highly recognized for her dedication to the community and is a six-time award recipient and well-rounded public speaker. Dr. Vaughn has also collaborated with MTV Networks regarding high school dropouts that included a follow-up appearance on Fox and Friends to discuss the importance of education and the epidemic of high school dropouts.

Through her personal struggles and set-backs as a single mother, it is her hope to deliver a powerful message of perseverance, hope, and courage to students, single moms and leaders across the world!

To learn more about Dr. Vaughn, please visit **www.drmv.net** or **www.teenandsinglemom.com.**

## Additional Readings by Dr. MV
## Purchase on **www.amazon.com** – or – **www.drmv.net**
## If You Can Birth a Baby, You Can Birth Your Dreams

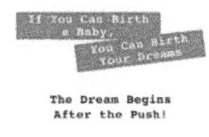

## BRIDE (Becoming Royal in Daddy's Eyes)

## Don't Grow Weary While Leading Booklet

www.ingramcontent.com/pod-product-compliance
Lightning Source LLC
Chambersburg PA
CBHW072040060426
42449CB00010BA/2375